REPTILES

ANIMALS IN DISGUISE

Lynn Stone

The Rourke Corporation, Inc.
Vero Beach, Florida 32964

PHOTO CREDITS
© Peter James: title page, pages 4, 15, 17; © Lynn M. Stone: cover, pages 7, 8, 10, 12, 13, 18, 21

EDITORIAL SERVICES:
Penworthy Learning Systems

Library of Congress Cataloging-in-Publication Data

Stone, Lynn M.
    Reptiles / Lynn M. Stone.
        p. cm. — (Animals in disguise)
    Includes index
    Summary: Describes how various reptiles use ways to disguise themselves and fool other animals, including camouflage, lures, and other tricks with color and shape.
    ISBN 0-86593-483-5
    1. Reptiles—Juvenile literature. 2. Camouflage (Biology) —Juvenile literature.
[1. Reptiles. 2. Camouflage (Biology)] I. Title II. Series. Stone, Lynn M.
Animals in disguise.
QL644.2.S756 1998
597.9'1472—dc21   98–6328
                                                                CIP
                                                                AC

Printed in the USA

TABLE OF CONTENTS

REPTILES

A **disguise** (dis GYZ) is a way of hiding who you really are. Many **reptiles** (REP tylz) use disguise to hide who they really are.

Reptiles are the snakes, lizards, turtles, alligators, crocodiles, and **tuatara** (too uh TAHR uh). Except for snakes and a few legless lizards, reptiles have four feet or flippers and toes with claws. Reptiles are dressed in scales or plates.

Reptiles have several ways to disguise themselves. With those disguises, they usually fool other animals.

The ball python hides its head by having it look like another tail.

STAYING ALIVE

Reptiles use disguises to keep themselves alive. Disguise helps a reptile that may be **prey** (PRAY), or food, hide from **predators** (PRED uh turz). Disguise can also help a predator, a hunting animal, hide from its prey.

Reptiles can be both predators and prey. The trick is to be a predator without becoming the prey.

No disguise is perfect, and this toad falls prey to a hognosed snake.

REPTILES IN DISGUISE

A reptile has to eat, find shelter, and find a mate. At the same time it doesn't want to become a meal for a predator. To work out the problem, many reptiles hide their real selves.

Hiding does not always mean crawling under a log. A good disguise can help a reptile hide without crawling anywhere.

Most reptile disguises depend upon color. The **cryptic** (KRIP tik) colors of the horned lizard, for example, make a wonderful disguise.

When this horned lizard stays perfectly still, it looks like the rocks around it.

CAMOUFLAGE

When the horned lizard lies still, it doesn't look like a lizard. It looks like the pebbly desert ground where it lives. Cryptic colors like the lizard's, match an animal's surroundings.

The lizard's disguise raises its chances of survival—staying alive. If it doesn't look like a lizard, a lizard-eating animal likely won't find it.

The lizard's disguise is simple **camouflage** (KAM uh FLAHJ). Camouflage is an animal's way of using its color to blend into its surroundings.

Cryptic coloring camouflages a fence lizard on a log.

By staying among green plants, a Carolina anole usually can eat without being eaten.

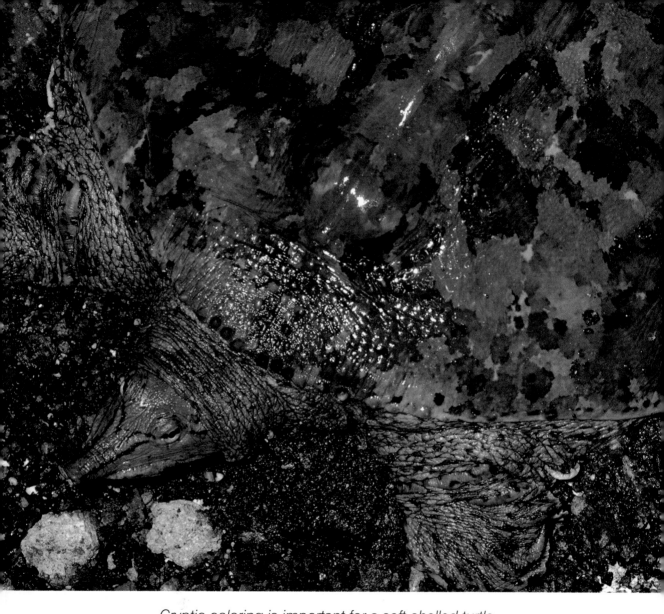

Cryptic coloring is important for a soft-shelled turtle.

TRICKS OF DISGUISE

Camouflage also helps reptile predators hide from their prey. If prey animals always saw their predators, they would almost always escape. The predator would soon die. In the animal world, the wins and losses of predator and prey balance each other.

Cryptic colors are one kind of disguise. Reptiles have other tricks, too. A certain turtle, for example, uses a bait. One kind of gecko has a tail shaped like a leaf (see first page).

The alligator snapping turtle's tongue looks like a wriggly worm and draws fish to the turtle's mouth.

TRICKS WITH COLOR

Most animals stay camouflaged only if they stay "home." The copperhead is well camouflaged when it stays on a bed of leaves. If the copperhead slithers onto a bed of moss, it loses its camouflage.

The chameleon, a lizard, has no problem moving from one place to another. It slowly changes its skin color to match different surroundings!

Not one to stand out in a crowd, the chameleon can almost always change its skin color to blend in.

SHAPES

Alligators and crocodiles can move quickly through the water. But they usually lie still. Their dark backs, long bodies, and stillness are all part of their disguise as floating logs.

Also, alligators and crocodiles have white bellies. When seen from below, those bellies are hard to see. That's because the water surface is bright. Fish use the same camouflage, with their dark backs and light undersides.

A big alligator camouflages itself in a mat of tiny duckweed plants.

MIMICS

Some reptiles disguise who they really are by looking like who they aren't. Consider the coral snake. It has a deadly bite. But it looks like two other snakes. One has only weak **venom** (VEN um), or poison. The other has no venom.

Maybe the true coral snake is copying, or **mimicking** (MIM ik ing), the one that has weak venom. A predator bitten by the false coral snake would always stay away from its look-alike.

The coral snake mimics look-alike snakes whose bite makes predators ill.

A TURTLE'S BAIT

Turtles wear colors that blend with their surroundings. The alligator snapping turtle, for example, can almost disappear. Its mossy back blends into the bottom of a pond. The alligator snapper's disguise doesn't end there, however.

As it waits, still as a stone, the snapper opens its mouth and wiggles its pink tongue. To a hungry fish, the tongue looks like a worm. When the fish tries to seize the "worm," the snapper quickly closes its mouth.

Glossary

camouflage (KAM uh FLAHJ) — the ability of an animal to use color, actions, and shape to blend into its surroundings

cryptic (KRIP tik) — that which helps hide, such as the colors of an animal that help it hide in its surroundings

disguise (dis GYZ) — a way of changing an animal's appearance

mimicking (MIM ik ing) — copying of actions or appearance of another

predator (PRED uh tur) — an animal that hunts other animals for food

prey (PRAY) — an animal that is hunted by other animals

reptiles (REP tylz) — the group of cold-blooded animals with backbones that are usually covered with scaly skin

tuatara (too uh TAHR uh) — an unusual reptile of lizardlike appearance found on a few islands off New Zealand

venom (VEN um) — a poison, made by certain snakes and other animals, for killing or injuring prey

INDEX

FURTHER READING:

Find out more about Animals in Disguise with these helpful books:
• Greenway, Theresa. *Jungle*. Knopf, 1994
• McCarthy, Colin. *Reptile*. Knopf, 1991
• Parker, Steve. *Natural World*. Knopf, 1994
• Smith, Trevor. *Amazing Lizards*. Knopf, 1990